Classic Bible Stories
for
Jewish Children

Classic Bible Stories
for
Jewish Children

Retold by
Alfred J. Kolatch

Illustrated by
Harry Araten

Jonathan David Publishers, Inc.
Middle Village, New York 11379

**Classic Bible Stories
for
Jewish Children**

Jonathan David Publishers, Inc.
68-22 Eliot Avenue
Middle Village, NY 11379

6 8 10 9 7 5

Library of Congress Cataloging-in-Publication Data

Kolatch, Alfred J.
    Classic Bible Stories for Jewish children/by Alfred J. Kolatch: Illustrated by Harry Araten
        p. cm.
    Summary: Twenty-four Old Testament stories about such familiar characters as Noah,
Joseph, Moses, David and Goliath, Ruth and Naomi, and Daniel.
    ISBN 0-8246-0362-1
    1. Bible stories, English—O.T. [1. Bible stories—O.T.]
I. Araten, Harry, ill. II. Title
BS551.2.k59 1993
221.9'505—dc20   93-10165
                                                                      CIP

                                                                        AC

Book design by Jennifer Vignone
Printed in China

To
Assaf
and all children
everywhere

Table of Contents

1. In the Very Beginning 8

2. Why the Snake Lost Its Legs 10

3. Cain: The Jealous Brother 12

4. Noah Builds an Ark 14

5. Noah Sees a Rainbow 16

6. Finding a Wife for Isaac 18

7. Joseph the Dreamer 20

8. Joseph Saves Egypt 22

9. The Israelites Become Slaves 24

10. A Princess Saves Baby Moses 26

11. Moses Shows His Courage 28

12. Moses and the Burning Bush 30

13. Miracle at the Sea 34

14. Moses Strikes the Rock 36

15. The Walls Came Tumbling Down 38

16. The Secret of Samson's Strength 40

17. David Battles a Giant 44

18. King Solomon Builds a Temple 48

19. Elijah: The Miracle Prophet 52

20. Jonah and the Big Fish 54

21. Ruth and Naomi 58

22. Mordecai Rides a Royal Horse 60

23. Three Friends in a Fiery Furnace 64

24. Daniel in the Lion's Den 66

In the Very Beginning

BEFORE **GOD CREATED THE** world, there was darkness and emptiness everywhere. There were no trees or plants. No animals or people. Only water covered the face of the earth.

God's voice suddenly boomed out: "Let there be light!" And there was light.

When God saw that the light was good, He separated the light from the darkness. God called the light Day, and he called the darkness Night. And so ended the first day of Creation.

In the five days that followed, God continued to create the world. He separated the waters to form oceans, seas, rivers and lakes. The dry land that then appeared was called Earth.

God said, "Now let the Earth bring forth plants, trees, and every kind of vegetation." And so it was.

And then God filled the seas and oceans with fish of every kind. And the dry land was filled with every kind of living creature: cattle, creeping things, birds and wild beasts.

God saw that what He had made was very good. But one thing was missing. God said to the angels, "Let us make man to rule over the fish of the seas, the birds of the sky, and all things that crawl on the Earth." And so man was created in the image of God.

יְהִי אוֹר

LET THERE BE LIGHT!

Genesis 1:3

The first man was called Adam, and the first woman was called Eve.

Adam and Eve became man and wife, and they lived together happily in a lovely place called the Garden of Eden.

Why the Snake Lost Its Legs

WHILE WALKING IN THE Garden of Eden, a snake, who in those days had legs like most other animals, saw Adam and Eve picking fruit from many different trees. The snake noticed that Adam and Eve did not touch the fruit that grew on one of the trees in the garden.

"Why haven't you picked the fruit of the Tree of Knowledge?" the snake asked Eve.

"Because God warned us not to eat the fruit of that tree," she answered.

"You don't know what you are missing," said the snake. "The fruit is juicy and delicious!"

The snake then reached up and picked a fruit from a branch of the forbidden tree.

"Take a bite," he said to Eve. "You'll love it!"

"No, I'm not supposed to," she replied. "God told us not to."

"Oh, come on!" the snake insisted. "Nothing will happen to you if you take just a tiny bite."

"All right. I'll try it," Eve finally agreed.

"It *is* delicious!" said Eve after biting into the fruit. "What kind of fruit is it?"

THE TREE OF LIFE AND THE TREE OF KNOWLEDGE

Genesis 2:9

"Who knows?" the snake shrugged. "It might be an apple or a fig. Or maybe an orange. I can't tell for sure. But the fruit is sweet and juicy, isn't it?"

"It is very tasty," said Eve. "But now I'm sorry I ate it. I disobeyed God. He told us not to eat fruit from the Tree of Knowledge."

When God saw how the snake had tricked Eve into tasting the forbidden fruit, He became very angry. "Because you have been so evil," God told the snake, "you will lose your legs!"

And from that time on all snakes have had to crawl on their bellies.

Cain: The Jealous Brother

ADAM AND EVE HAD two sons: Cain and Abel. Cain, the elder brother, was a farmer. Abel was a shepherd.

One day, the two brothers offered gifts to God. Cain brought a basket of fruits and vegetables that he had grown on his land. Abel brought the best sheep of his flock.

For some unknown reason, God liked Abel's gift more than the offering brought by Cain. This made Cain very angry.

The more Cain thought about it, the more furious he became. Finally, one day, when both brothers were out in the field, Cain attacked his brother and killed him.

God said to Cain: "I have been looking for your brother. Where is Abel?"

הֲשׁוֹמֵר אָחִי אָנֹכִי?

AM I MY BROTHER'S KEEPER?

Genesis 4:9

"I do not know! Am I my brother's keeper?" answered Cain.

God knew that Cain was not telling the truth. "Cain, because you were jealous of your brother and murdered him, and because you lied, you shall be punished," God said. "You shall no longer have a place that you can call home."

And so, for the rest of his life Cain was a wanderer on the face of the earth.

Noah Builds an Ark

WHEN GOD CREATED THE world, He hoped that the people who lived in it would be kind to each other.

But God was disappointed. He found that most people were selfish and greedy. They didn't care about anyone but themselves.

Of all the people on earth, only Noah was righteous.

God said to Noah: "I have decided to destroy the whole world and begin all over again."

God then commanded: "Noah, build an ark and bring into it your entire family and also two animals of every kind, one male and one female. You and your family and the animals in the ark will all be saved."

Noah began working immediately. He collected wood and built a large ark with many compartments. He carefully covered the ark, inside and outside, with tar. As soon as the ark was completed, Noah gathered his wife, his sons and their wives, and all the animals into it. And then the rain began to fall.

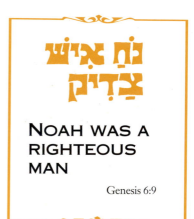

נֹחַ אִישׁ צַדִּיק

NOAH WAS A RIGHTEOUS MAN

Genesis 6:9

The rain continued for forty days and forty nights, and soon the whole earth was flooded. Every house, every tree, even the highest mountain was under water.

The wind blew fiercely, but Noah's ark kept floating on the water. All living things outside the ark had died. And just as God had promised, Noah, his family, and the animals inside the ark were saved.

Noah Sees a Rainbow

AFTER ONE HUNDRED AND fifty days, Noah's ark came to rest on the top of Mount Ararat, in the country we today call Turkey.

Noah opened a window of the ark and sent out a raven. He knew that the raven, with its powerful beak, could break off a branch from a tree and bring it back to him. This would prove that the water no longer covered the trees and that it was safe for everyone to leave the ark and start a new life.

The raven left the ark but never returned.

Noah then sent out a dove, and the dove returned with an olive branch in its beak. Noah knew that olive trees do not grow on top of mountains, so he felt sure that the flood waters had begun to go down.

God spoke to Noah and said, "Come out of the ark together with your family and all the birds and animals." Noah did as he was instructed.

Then God saw all the ruin that had come to the world that he had created. "Never again will I destroy the earth because of man's evil ways," God promised.

וַיְשַׁלַּח אֶת הַיּוֹנָה

AND HE SENT FORTH THE DOVE

Genesis 8:8

And as a sign of His promise, a rainbow of blue, green, red, yellow, and many other beautiful colors appeared in the sky.

"From now on," God said to Noah, "whenever I see a rainbow in the sky, I will remember My promise to never again destroy the earth."

Finding a Wife for Isaac

ABRAHAM WAS GETTING old, and he worried about his son Isaac. Isaac was not yet married.

Abraham lived in the Land of Canaan, the land now called Israel. His neighbors, the Canaanites, worshiped idols, and Abraham did not want his son to marry a girl from a family of idol worshippers.

The only place to find a wife for Isaac is in the faraway Land of Ur, where my relatives live, thought Abraham. Ur was a town in present-day Iraq.

Abraham said to his trusted servant, Eliezer, "Go to Ur and find the right girl to be Isaac's wife."

"What if the girl I find refuses to come back with me?" asked Eliezer. "What if she will not leave her family? Should I take Isaac to her, to live in Ur?"

"No," said Abraham. "Absolutely not! If she is the right girl for Isaac, she will come back with you."

Eliezer packed his bags and left to find a wife for Isaac. When he reached the outskirts of Ur, Eliezer settled down with his camels near the town's well. He waited there until sundown, when young maidens would come to fetch water for their families.

שְׁתֵה וְגַם גְּמַלֶּיךָ אַשְׁקֶה

DRINK, AND I WILL ALSO GIVE WATER TO YOUR CAMELS

Genesis 24:14

Eliezer watched one girl after another as she drew water from the well. One beautiful girl attracted his attention.

"Please, may I have a drink of water?" Eliezer asked.

"Drink, my lord," she answered without hesitation. "Drink as much as you wish, and when you are finished, I will draw water for your camels."

What a lovely girl! thought Eliezer. "What is your name?" he asked.

"Rebecca," she answered shyly.

After the two talked for a while, Eliezer discovered that Rebecca was the granddaughter of Nachor, Abraham's brother. She was a member of Abraham's family!

What luck! Eliezer thought. *She is the perfect wife for my master's son!*

Rebecca took Eliezer to meet her family.

"I would like to take Rebecca to Canaan to marry my master's son," Eliezer said to them.

Eliezer then turned to the beautiful Rebecca. "Will you come with me to the Land of Canaan?" he asked.

"Yes, I will," Rebecca answered happily.

Rebecca's family blessed her and prepared her for the journey to the Land of Canaan, where she would meet Isaac and become his wife.

Joseph the Dreamer

JACOB HAD TWELVE SONS and one daughter. Of all his children, Joseph was Jacob's favorite.

Father Jacob loved Joseph so much that he gave him a handsome coat of many colors. When the brothers saw the beautiful gift Joseph had received, they became very jealous.

One night, Joseph had an unusual dream.

"I dreamed," Joseph said to his brothers, "that we were all standing out in the field tying up bundles of grain. Suddenly, my bundle stood up straight and all of your bundles bowed down to mine."

When the brothers heard this dream, they were furious. "Joseph, what kind of dream is that?" they demanded. "Do you hope to be our master?"

Joseph was silent.

Weeks later, Joseph told his brothers about another dream. "Last night," he said, "I dreamed that the sun, the moon, and eleven stars bowed down to me."

הִנֵּה בַּעַל הַחֲלֹמוֹת בָּא

BEHOLD! HERE COMES THE DREAMER!

Genesis 37:19

The brothers knew immediately what this dream meant. The sun was their father, the moon their mother. And the eleven stars were Joseph's eleven brothers.

"What are you trying to say?" the brothers shouted at Joseph. "Do you want to rule over us? Do you want us to bow down to you?"

And from that time on, whenever the brothers saw Joseph coming, they snickered, "Behold! Here comes the dreamer! Here comes Joseph, the dreamer!"

Soon thereafter, the brothers sold Joseph to a caravan of Ishmaelites. The Ishmaelites took Joseph to Egypt and sold him there as a slave.

Joseph Saves Egypt

PHARAOH, AS THE KING of Egypt was called, had a dream. In his dream, the king saw seven fine, healthy cows grazing in a green field near the Nile River. Suddenly, seven scrawny, sickly cows came up from the Nile and ate the healthy cows. Pharaoh awoke abruptly.

What a strange dream! Pharaoh thought to himself. And then he went back to sleep.

A short time later, the king had another dream.

In this dream Pharaoh saw seven thick, healthy ears of grain growing on a single stalk. Close behind these healthy ears of grain grew seven thin, dry ears. Suddenly, the thin ears swallowed up the healthy ones.

Again, Pharaoh awoke abruptly. *What do these strange dreams mean?* he wondered.

Pharaoh summoned the wisest men in the entire Land of Egypt to his palace. The king described his dreams to them. "Explain to me what they mean," he demanded.

אֵין נָבוֹן
וְחָכָם כָּמוֹךָ

NO ONE IS
AS WISE
AND SMART
AS YOU

Genesis 41:39

But not one of the wise men could answer.

Then, the king's butler spoke up. "When I was in jail," he said, "I met a young Hebrew named Joseph who was also a prisoner. He was able to explain the meaning of some of my dreams."

Pharaoh sent for Joseph immediately.

When the young man stood before the king, the Egyptian ruler described his dreams. Joseph listened carefully.

Then, slowly, Joseph explained: "Your Majesty, both dreams are really one. They mean that the next seven years will be good, healthy ones for Egypt. There will be plenty of food for everyone. But after that there will be seven years of hunger. There will be a famine in the land. All the food from the seven good years will be used up, and there will not be enough food for everyone."

"What should I do?" Pharaoh asked eagerly.

"Your Majesty," advised Joseph, "should appoint a wise man to be in charge of collecting food during the seven good years, and that food should be saved to be eaten only during the seven years of famine."

Pharaoh was very pleased with Joseph's advice.

"I appoint you to carry out the plan and prepare Egypt for the seven years of famine," said Pharaoh. "I know of no one as wise and as smart as you in the entire Land of Egypt."

And so, Joseph became assistant to the king. For seven years he stored extra grain in warehouses. And when the seven good years had ended, there was enough food stored away to save the people of Egypt from hunger.

The Israelites Become Slaves

SECOND ONLY TO the king, Joseph was the most important man in the Land of Egypt.

Joseph wanted his father, Jacob, and the rest of the family to move to Egypt so they could be together. Jacob agreed and the family made the long journey from Canaan to Egypt.

Jacob's family settled in Goshen, a beautiful place with rich soil that was excellent for farming. There, they raised sheep and cattle and grew many different kinds of vegetables.

As the years passed, the families of Jacob's sons grew larger and larger. The Israelites, as the descendants of Jacob were then called, became a very powerful people.

After Joseph died, a new king became the Pharaoh of Egypt. He did not know of Joseph and what he had done to save the country from famine. The new Pharaoh was only worried about how rich and powerful the Israelites had become.

וַיָּקָם מֶלֶךְ חָדָשׁ עַל מִצְרָיִם

AND A NEW KING AROSE IN EGYPT

Exodus 1:8

"How can I be certain that I can trust these people?" the king said to his advisors. "What if war comes? What if an enemy attacks us? How can we be sure that the Israelites—the Children of Israel—will fight on our side? Maybe they will join the enemy and fight against us!"

The king decided that it would be best if the Children of Israel were to become his slaves.

"Make them work hard building pyramids," Pharaoh commanded his officers. "And tell them to build thick brick walls around the cities where we store our grain and ammunition."

"Order them to make their own bricks. And don't supply them with the straw they need to make the bricks," Pharaoh added. "Let them go out into the fields and find it themselves."

Life for the Israelites in Egypt became unbearable. For long hours each day they were forced to slave under the blazing hot sun.

The Children of Israel hoped and prayed for someone to set them free. And before long, a leader named Moses appeared.

A Princess Saves Baby Moses

EVEN AFTER THE KING of Egypt had made the Israelites his slaves, they continued to grow in number. And the harder the Israelites worked, the stronger they became.

Pharaoh was terribly worried. "Kill all Hebrew boys as soon as they are born," he commanded. "Throw them into the Nile River. Allow only the girls to live!"

When one Hebrew couple—Amram and Jochebed—became the parents of a baby boy, they decided to hide the child in their house. Luckily, when Pharaoh's soldiers searched the house, the baby did not cry and the soldiers did not find him.

But after three months, Jochebed decided that it was no longer safe to keep the baby boy at home. *His voice is stronger now. He can be heard far away when he cries*, she thought.

So Jochebed placed her son in a straw basket and hid him among the thick green reeds along the banks of the Nile.

EVERY BOY WHO IS BORN SHALL YOU CAST INTO THE RIVER

Exodus 1:22

Jochebed then said to her daughter: "Miriam, I want you to stand guard. Make sure that no one sees you, but keep watch over your baby brother in the basket. Make sure that no harm comes to him."

One morning, Miriam watched as the princess, daughter of Pharaoh, came down to the river to bathe. Suddenly, the princess noticed a basket floating on the water. "Go fetch that basket and bring it to me!" she ordered her maid.

The maid brought the straw basket to the princess. And when the princess lifted the cover, a baby started crying.

"This must be a Hebrew child," she said. "Who else would hide a baby in a river? Such a sweet child! I must take him back to the palace."

When Miriam saw what the princess had done, she rushed to her side:

"Would you like me to find a Hebrew nurse to care for this child?" she asked.

"Yes, that would be wonderful," responded Pharaoh's daughter.

Miriam quickly ran home and brought her mother, Jochebed, to the princess.

"Please, take this child to your home and care for it until it is older," the princess said to Jochebed. "I will pay your wages."

Jochebed took the child, her own baby boy, and nursed him.

When the child was older, she brought him back to the princess, who loved the child very much and adopted him as her son. Pharaoh's daughter remembered how her maid had drawn the child out of the water, and so she named him Moses, which means "drawn out of the water."

Moses Shows His Courage

BABY MOSES WAS RAISED like a prince in the palace of King Pharaoh. But he never forgot that he was a Hebrew, one of the Children of Israel.

One day, when Moses was already a powerful young man, he watched the Hebrew slaves as they made bricks under the broiling sun.

Suddenly, Moses heard one of the Egyptian guards screaming at a slave, "Why are you working so slowly? Get a move on you!" And then the guard began beating the Hebrew slave viciously.

Moses was filled with rage. He rushed up to the guard. "How dare you treat a man that way!" he cried out. And then Moses struck the guard and beat him until he was dead.

When King Pharaoh was told what Moses had done to the Egyptian guard, he said to his officers, "Go find Moses and kill him!"

When Moses heard about the king's order, he ran off into the desert to the Land of Midian.

Moses was lonely and depressed. He sat down near a well and wondered what to do. "Where shall I go? I feel like a stranger in a strange land."

וַיִּפֶן כֹּה וָכֹה
וַיַּרְא כִּי אֵין
אִישׁ

AND HE
LOOKED
THIS WAY
AND THAT
WAY AND
SAW
NO ONE

Exodus 2:12

Just then, seven young sisters came to the well to fetch water for their sheep. But a group of shepherds came up behind the girls and chased them away. "This is our well," they said. "Go find your own!"

Moses stood up quickly and challenged the shepherds: "Begone! Leave these girls alone, or you will have to deal with me."

The shepherds were afraid of the muscular stranger. Quickly, they picked up their water buckets and ran off into the fields. Moses then drew water from the well and watered the flocks of the seven sisters.

When the girls returned home, their father, Jethro, said to them, "How is it that you have returned so early today?"

"An Egyptian man rescued us from the shepherds," they explained. "He even drew water from the well and watered our sheep."

"Where is this man?" asked Jethro. "Why didn't you bring him back to have a meal with us?"

The girls went back to the well hoping to find Moses. Moses was still there.

"We would like to invite you to come back to our house," they said to him. "Father wants you to be our guest."

Moses went home with the seven sisters. He introduced himself to their father and told him all about his escape from Egypt.

Jethro was very impressed by the courage of Moses, and he gave Moses his daughter Tzipporah as a wife. Moses was no longer a stranger in a strange land.

Moses and the Burning Bush

WHILE LIVING IN MIDIAN with his wife Tzipporah, Moses kept busy tending the flocks of his father-in-law, Jethro. One day, he took the sheep far out into the wilderness to a place called Horeb, the Mountain of God.

Suddenly, out of nowhere, an angel of the Lord appeared to Moses in a bush that was ablaze with fire.

Moses couldn't believe his eyes. "Why does the bush keep burning but not burn up?" he asked himself.

When God saw the puzzled look on Moses' face, He called out to him from the bush: "Moses! Moses!"

"Here I am," answered Moses.

"Come no closer," God said. "Remove the sandals from your feet, for the land on which you are standing is holy ground."

Moses did as God commanded.

וְהַסְּנֶה אֵינֶנּוּ אֻכָּל

AND THE BUSH DID NOT BURN UP

Exodus 3:2

God then continued to speak: "I know well about the suffering of My people in Egypt. I have heard their cries for help. I have come down to save them. Moses, I want you to help Me."

"You want *me* to help *You!*" said Moses. "I am just a plain man. How can I help You?"

"Go with your brother, Aaron, to Pharaoh," God ordered, "and tell him that he must free the Israelites."

Moses was terrified. "Am I important enough," he said to God, "that I should go to Pharaoh and demand that he free the Israelites from Egypt? Pharaoh will not listen to me."

"Do not be afraid," God said. "I will be with you."

So Moses, together with his brother, Aaron, went to Pharaoh's palace to see the mighty king of Egypt.

"Let my people go!" Moses demanded. "Let my people go free so that they may worship our God."

"No!" replied Pharaoh. "The Israelites are my slaves. They may not leave Egypt!"

Moses and Aaron were unhappy as they left the palace.

Moses turned to God. "What shall I do?" he pleaded. "Pharaoh will pay no attention to me!"

God answered: "Go once again to Pharaoh and say to him, 'If you do not free the Children of Israel, my God will punish you and all the Egyptian people.'"

Moses went back to see the king and told him what God had said.

Once again, Pharaoh ignored Moses.

God then said to Moses, "Tell your brother, Aaron, to take his staff and to hold it out over the waters of Egypt."

Aaron went to the Nile River and stretched out his staff over the waters. Pharaoh and all the members of his court watched as suddenly the waters turned to blood.

All the fish in the river died, and a terrible smell arose from the waters.

But Pharaoh was not frightened by this horrible plague. He still refused to set the Israelites free.

So God sent a second plague, the plague of frogs. The Nile was swarming with frogs. Frogs were everywhere in the king's palace.

And then came a third plague, the plague of lice.

And then came the plague of wild beasts, and then the plague of locusts.

All in all, ten terrifying plagues were sent upon the Egyptians.

Finally, Pharaoh could stand it no longer. "Go! Take your people and leave the country," the Egyptian leader said to Moses. "Go, worship your God in the desert!"

The Israelites quickly gathered up their belongings and fled Egypt.

The Children of Israel were free at last!

Miracle at the Sea

SOON AFTER PHARAOH gave the Children of Israel permission to leave Egypt, he changed his mind.

"I made an awful mistake," the king said to his advisors. "Chase after the Israelites, and when you catch up with them, take them prisoner and bring them back to Egypt."

By this time, the Israelites were making their way slowly through the desert. They could not move quickly because of the many children and elderly people among them.

Suddenly, the Children of Israel heard the pounding of horses' hooves and the spinning wheels of chariots behind them. When they turned around, they saw Pharaoh's army approaching rapidly.

The Israelites panicked. The Egyptians were behind them and the Sea of Reeds was in front of them.

"What have you done to us?" the Israelites demanded of Moses. "The Egyptians will bury us in the desert."

"Do not fear!" said Moses. "God is on our side. He will perform a miracle!"

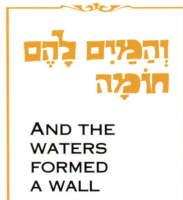

וְהַמַּיִם לָהֶם חוֹמָה

AND THE WATERS FORMED A WALL

Exodus 14:22

Moses raised his rod and held it out over the sea. The water spread apart and stood up like two solid walls. In between, the land was dry.

"Follow me," Moses said as he stepped into the sea and walked between the two columns of water.

Quickly, the Children of Israel followed. And soon all the Israelites had reached the other side of the sea.

Close behind, riding between the two walls of water, were the Egyptian horsemen and their hundreds of chariots. But before the Egyptians could reach the other side of the sea, the two walls of water collapsed, and all the king's soldiers and their horses and chariots were covered by water.

"We are saved!" the Israelites shouted happily. "God has saved us!"

Miriam, the sister of Moses, then took out her tambourine and began to tap out happy tunes. Other women joined Miriam, and everyone jumped for joy and danced and sang a song of thanks to God.

Moses Strikes the Rock

AGAIN AND AGAIN GOD had assured Moses, "I will free you from Egyptian slavery, and I will bring you to the land which I promised to Abraham, Isaac, and Jacob."

And now, free at last, the Children of Israel began the long march to the Promised Land, to Canaan, to that special land that was later called Palestine and is now called Israel.

The journey through the desert was very difficult. The days were very hot and the nights very cold, and the Israelites were thirsty and hungry and very tired.

"We need water to drink," the people begged.

Moses turned to God. "Your people, the Children of Israel, are thirsty," he pleaded. "They need water. Please, please help them!"

God pointed to a huge rock and said, "Talk to the rock and it will send out water."

Moses walked over to the rock and, instead of talking to the rock as God had instructed, he struck it with his staff.

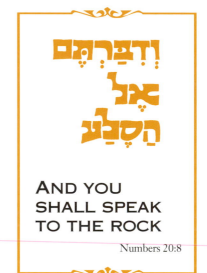

וְדִבַּרְתֶּם אֶל הַסֶּלַע

AND YOU SHALL SPEAK TO THE ROCK

Numbers 20:8

God saw what Moses had done. "Moses, because you have disobeyed me," He said, "you may not enter the Promised Land!"

Moses was heartbroken. Looking past the Jordan River, in the distance he could see the City of Jericho in the Land of Canaan.

"This is the land that I promised to Abraham, Isaac, and Jacob," God said to Moses. "I am allowing you to see it with your own eyes, but you shall not walk on its soil. This is the price you have to pay for disobeying me by striking the rock."

And so it was. At the age of 120, Moses died without ever setting foot on the land that God had promised to the children of Abraham, Isaac, and Jacob.

The Walls Came Tumbling Down

AFTER MOSES DIED, Joshua became the leader of Israel.

Joshua's first task was to lead the Israelites across the Jordan River in order to conquer the Land of Canaan.

He decided to send spies to Jericho, the city on the other side of the river, in order to find out how difficult it might be to capture the city.

One dark night, the spies crossed the river and discovered that Jericho was surrounded by two thick walls. They sneaked into the city and learned that the people living there were strong and able warriors.

The spies returned to Joshua and reported what they had seen. "How, then," Joshua asked, "shall we enter the city to capture it?"

"Dig a tunnel under the walls," suggested one advisor.

"Don't let any food enter the city," said another. "The people will grow weak and surrender."

"Let us pound away at the walls until they fall," suggested a third advisor.

"No, no, don't be foolish!" said Joshua. "These ideas won't work. We need a better way. We need a miracle!"

Joshua turned to God. "Help us, O Lord!" he cried out. "What shall we do?"

וַתִּפֹּל
הַחוֹמָה
תַּחְתֶּיהָ

AND THE WALLS CAME TUMBLING DOWN

Joshua 6:20

God answered, "Let seven priests take seven rams' horns and march around the walls of Jericho every day for six days. Behind them, let other priests carry the Holy Ark containing the Ten Commandments. And behind them, let all the soldiers follow."

God continued to instruct Joshua: "On the seventh day, as the priests blow on their horns, everyone in the procession is to march around the walls of the City of Jericho seven times. Then, let one long blast be sounded from one horn."

Joshua followed God's instructions. And, behold, when the final long blast of the horn was sounded, the mighty walls of Jericho came tumbling down!

The Secret of Samson's Strength

MANOACH WAS A member of the tribe of Dan, one of the twelve tribes of Israel. He and his wife had no children.

One day, an angel appeared before Manoach's wife. "You will soon give birth to a son," the angel announced, "and he will save Israel from the Philistines."

"However," the angel continued, "you must be careful not to drink wine or eat food that is unclean. And when your child is born, do not cut the hair on his head. Raise him to serve God."

Within the year, a son was born to Manoach and his wife. The child, who was named Samson, grew up to be so strong and courageous that the Israelites made him their leader.

Samson was not afraid of anyone or anything. Once, when a full-grown lion came roaring towards him, he tore the wild animal apart with his bare hands.

On another occasion, to punish the Philistines, Israel's enemy, Samson caught three hundred foxes and put a torch to their tails. He set the animals loose in the middle of a field of grain belonging to the Philistines. The foxes ran wildly back and forth and the crops caught fire and were destroyed.

פְּלִשְׁתִּים
עָלֶיךָ
שִׁמְשׁוֹן

SAMSON, THE PHILISTINES ARE COMING AFTER YOU

Judges 16:20

The Philistines wanted to kill Samson. But they could not figure out how to capture him.

One day, Samson met a beautiful Philistine girl named Delilah. He found her very attractive.

When the Philistine leaders learned that Samson, the strong man of Israel, was in love with a Philistine girl, they were delighted. *She might be able to help us*, they thought.

The leaders approached Delilah. "You are one of us," they said. "You must help us discover the secret of Samson's strength. Do it for your people! We need your help!"

"I will try," Delilah promised.

But as hard as Delilah tried to make Samson reveal the secret, he refused to do so.

Day after day, Delilah nagged Samson. "How can you say you love me," she would say over and over again, "if you will not tell me what makes you so strong?"

Finally, in a moment of weakness, Samson said to Delilah: "My secret is that no razor has ever touched my head. If my hair were cut, I would lose my strength. I would be no stronger than an ordinary man."

Immediately, Delilah sent a message to the Philistines telling them that she now knew Samson's secret and requesting them to come to her at once.

While waiting for the Philistines to arrive, Delilah rested Samson's head on her lap, and soon the powerful leader of the Israelites fell asleep.

When the Philistines arrived, Delilah told one of them to cut off the seven locks of hair on Samson's head.

When Samson awoke, he found that his strength was completely gone. The Philistines grabbed Samson, blinded him, put him in chains, and threw him into prison.

One day, after Samson's hair had begun to grow back, the Philistines gathered in front of their temple to celebrate the victory over their bitter enemy. They decided to bring Samson out of prison so that they might make fun of him by having him dance before them.

After performing for the Philistines, Samson said to his guard: "I am very weary. Let me lean upon the pillars of your temple so that I may rest."

Samson then stretched out his arms, placed them on two of the huge temple pillars, and prayed: "O Lord, my God! Give me strength just this once!"

Then, with all his might, Samson pushed against the pillars and the Philistine temple came crashing to the ground, killing Samson and everyone who had assembled there.

David Battles a Giant

A HUGE, SCARY-LOOKING Philistine named Goliath shouted at the Israelites from the top of a hill, "Why don't you come and fight me? Ha! Are you afraid?"

The Israelites trembled as they heard the challenge from the lips of this giant who stood more than nine feet tall.

"If the man you choose kills me," Goliath continued, "then my people, the Philistines, will become your slaves. But if I kill your man, you will become our slaves!"

Just then, a small young shepherd boy named David appeared in the army camp of the Israelites. David had come to see his brothers, who were serving as soldiers in King Saul's army.

David heard Goliath's challenge and thought for a moment. Then, he said, "King Saul, let me go and fight him."

הַכֶלֶב אָנֹכִי כִּי אַתָּה בָא אֵלַי בַּמַּקְלוֹת?

AM I A DOG THAT YOU COME AFTER ME WITH STICKS?

I Samuel 17:43

"Don't be foolish! You can't fight him," laughed the king. "You are only a boy. He is a powerful man. He is a warrior."

"Please! Allow me to fight the Philistine," David pleaded. "I am not afraid. I have killed lions and bears who were attacking my sheep. God, who protected me from the lion and the bear, will also save me from the Philistine giant!"

King Saul finally agreed. "Go! Fight the giant!" he said. "And may God be with you."

Saul then dressed David with a bronze helmet, a breastplate, and a sword. "I cannot even walk with all this heavy equipment," David protested.

David removed the helmet and breastplate, and cast aside the heavy sword. He picked up five smooth stones and put them in the pocket of his shepherd's pouch. Holding only a slingshot made of sticks in one hand, he went to meet Goliath.

When the giant saw little David coming toward him without a helmet or a breastplate or a sword, he howled. "Am I a dog that you come to fight me with sticks? Come here, little one," he roared, "and I will give your flesh to the birds of the air and the beasts of the field."

David was not scared. "You come to me with a sword and a spear," he said to Goliath, "but I come to you in the name of the Lord. God will deliver you into my hands."

David then drew one smooth stone from his pouch and placed it in the slingshot. He aimed it at the giant. The stone whizzed through the air and sank into Goliath's forehead. With a loud crash the giant fell to the ground. He was dead.

The Philistine soldiers fled, and the Israelites cheered their new hero, David, who was to become King of Israel.

King Solomon Builds a Temple

KING DAVID SPENT MOST of his years fighting the Philistines and other enemies of Israel. When David died and his son, Solomon, became king, the Land of Israel was at peace.

Solomon was a gentle man who loved nature and all kinds of animals. He especially loved horses because they were so strong and graceful. In his stable, Solomon had more than one thousand horses, many of whom competed in races held in the large stadium in Jerusalem. As many as ten thousand people attended these exciting events.

But there was one thing that Solomon wanted to do more than anything else. He wanted to build a magnificent Temple to honor God.

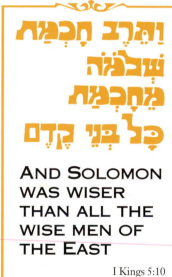

וַתֵּרֶב חָכְמַת שְׁלֹמֹה מֵחָכְמַת כָּל בְּנֵי קֶדֶם

AND SOLOMON WAS WISER THAN ALL THE WISE MEN OF THE EAST

I Kings 5:10

To build the Temple, Solomon knew that he would need strong cedar and cypress wood. So, he turned for help to King Hiram of Tyre, which is in the country now called Lebanon.

Solomon said to Hiram: "You know that my father could not build a Temple in honor of God because he was so busy battling the many enemies of Israel. But now we are at peace, and I want to build a Temple."

"Your father was my good friend," said Hiram. "I will do anything for his son."

"King Hiram, your country has beautiful cedar and cypress trees in the mountains of Lebanon," Solomon replied. "I will need strong timber to build God's house. Nowhere are there trees better than the cedars of Lebanon."

"Solomon, you can have as much timber as you wish," Hiram promised. "I will have trees cut down, and I will float them on rafts down the Mediterranean Sea to any place you desire."

Solomon was very grateful. "I will pay you for everything with wheat and oil," he said.

Hiram's workers began cutting down trees and floating them downstream so they could be brought to Jerusalem, where the Temple was to be built.

Solomon also needed blocks of stone for the Temple walls. In the hills of northern Israel he found large stone deposits, and he hired experienced masons to cut blocks of stone out of the mountainside.

More than 180,000 laborers were assigned by Solomon to work on the Temple. And after seven long years of backbreaking work, the building was completed.

King Solomon called the happy people of Jerusalem to come and stand in front of the magnificent Temple. He raised his hands toward Heaven and prayed:

> O Lord, God of Israel, who is in the heavens
> above and on the earth below, there is no God
> like you. We dedicate this beautiful house to You.

Elijah: The Miracle Prophet

ELIJAH WAS A VERY wise man and one of Israel's most courageous prophets. And like all prophets, he scolded the people when they misbehaved.

Elijah was afraid of no one, not even Ahab, King of Israel. When Elijah learned that King Ahab and his evil wife, Queen Jezebel, were worshiping idols, he reprimanded them.

"Why are you praying to idols?" Elijah asked. "Why do you not pray to the God of Israel? You will be punished!"

Ahab was very disturbed by Elijah's criticism. After Elijah left, the King ordered his soldiers to pursue the prophet and put him to death.

God called out to Elijah: "Hurry! Leave this place! Run off into the desert!"

"But how will I live there?" asked Elijah. "I will die of thirst in the hot, dry desert."

"Do not worry, Elijah. Water will be provided for you," God assured him.

"And where will I find food in the desert?" Elijah asked.

הָעֹרְבִים צִוִּיתִי לְכַלְכֶּלְךָ

I HAVE COMMANDED THE RAVENS TO FEED YOU

I Kings 17:4

"I have instructed the ravens to bring you food," God answered.

And so, Elijah went off to live in the desert. Every morning and evening, the ravens brought the prophet bread and meat. And from the desert wells Elijah was able to draw as much water as he needed.

But then, without warning, the wells went dry. Elijah looked everywhere but could find no water. The prophet wandered about aimlessly until, one day, he came upon the house of a widow living with her young son.

"Please, may I have some water?" Elijah begged. "And perhaps you can spare a small piece of bread. I am so hungry."

"I have no bread in the house," said the widow. "I promise you. I have noth-

52

ing but a handful of flour and a little bit of oil!"

"Go and make a small bread and bring it to me," Elijah replied. "And then make some breads for yourself and your son."

"But, I told you, I have only a small amount of flour and a tiny bit of oil," explained the widow. "How can I make so many breads?"

"Have faith!" Elijah said. "Do as I tell you."

The widow did as Elijah had suggested. And, miraculously, from a small amount of flour and tiny bit of oil she was able to bake enough bread to feed Elijah, her son, and herself for a long time.

Jonah and the Big Fish

ONE DAY ABOUT 2,700 years ago, God said to Jonah the prophet, "Go to the City of Nineveh! Tell the wicked people there that if they do not improve their behavior, the city will be destroyed and everyone in it will perish."

Jonah refused to do as God had commanded. He knew that God would not actually destroy the entire city just because some of its people were bad. And he was worried that if God did not destroy the city, the people would call him a liar, a false prophet.

Instead of going to Nineveh, Jonah boarded a large boat headed for Tarshish, a city far from Nineveh.

While Jonah was on the ship, a great storm blew up. The boat rocked and rolled violently, and the sailors were afraid that the boat would surely sink.

"There must be a passenger on this boat who is the cause of this storm!" one of the sailors cried out. "Let us find out who it is!"

The sailors carefully searched the boat, but they found no one who might be the cause of the storm. Then, they went to search the very lowest part of the boat where the cargo is held. And there they found Jonah fast asleep.

"Who are you?" the sailors asked him. "What are you doing here?"

"I am a Hebrew," the prophet replied. "I worship the Lord, God of Heaven, who made both the sea and the land."

"But why are you on this boat?" they demanded.

"I am running away from my God," Jonah answered. "I cannot do what He ordered."

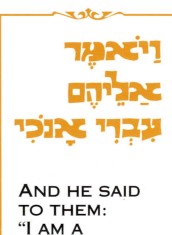

וַיֹּאמֶר אֲלֵיהֶם עִבְרִי אָנֹכִי

AND HE SAID TO THEM: "I AM A HEBREW."

Jonah 1:9

"That is why our boat is about to sink," said the sailors. "Jonah, please tell us what to do to calm the sea."

"Throw me overboard!" said Jonah. "Then the stormy sea will become calm."

Without waiting another second, the sailors picked up the prophet and hurled him overboard. And as soon as Jonah's body touched the water, the raging sea became quiet.

Jonah was in the water no longer than a few minutes when a huge fish the size of a whale swam toward him. Suddenly, the fish opened its mouth wide and swallowed Jonah in one gulp.

"Dear God, please save me!" cried Jonah. "I promise that from now on I will obey You."

God pitied Jonah. "Spit Jonah out onto dry land!" He ordered the fish.

The fish did as God had commanded.

Then, God ordered Jonah once again: "Go immediately to the great City of Nineveh and warn the people that they must change their bad behavior."

This time, Jonah obeyed. He traveled to Nineveh and announced to the people: "Stop your evil ways! If you refuse, in forty days your city will be destroyed!"

The people of Nineveh believed that Jonah was speaking in the name of God. The king told everyone to start fasting and to pray for forgiveness.

When God saw that the people of Nineveh were willing to change their evil ways, He was very pleased. And because they promised to lead good lives, God did not punish them.

Ruth and Naomi

THERE WAS NO FOOD in Bethlehem and other parts of the Land of Canaan, and the people were suffering greatly.

A man named Elimelech said to his wife, Naomi, "Let us move to the other side of the Jordan River, to the land of Moab. There, we will find food."

Elimelech, Naomi, and their two sons moved to Moab, and for a while they were happy. But then Elimelech died, leaving Naomi alone to raise the two young boys.

When the children grew up, they fell in love and married two girls from Moab. One girl was named Orpah and the other Ruth.

Ten years later, Naomi's sons died. Orpah and Ruth were left without husbands.

When the famine in Canaan ended, Naomi decided to move back to Bethlehem, where members of her family still lived.

"You stay here in Moab with your families," Naomi told her daughters-in-law. "Here, you will find new husbands."

כִּי אֶל אֲשֶׁר תֵּלְכִי אֵלֵךְ

FOR WHEREVER YOU GO, I WILL GO

Ruth 1:16

"Yes," Orpah said, "I will remain here in Moab."

But Ruth loved Naomi very much. "Naomi, I do not want to leave you," Ruth said. "I always want to be near you. I will go with you to Bethlehem."

"Please, Ruth, stay here," Naomi requested. "It will be better for you to remain in your homeland."

"No," Ruth insisted. "I love you. I cannot leave you. Where you go, I will go. Where you live, I will live. Your people will be my people, and your God my God. Where you die, I will die. And that is where I will be buried."

Tears streamed down Naomi's face as she listened to the loving words of her daughter-in-law.

Naomi took Ruth by the hand, and together they set out for the City of Bethlehem.

Mordecai Rides a Royal Horse

ABOUT 2,500 YEARS ago, in the city of Shushan in a country called Persia (which today is Iran), two palace guards planned to kill King Ahasueros.

A Jewish man named Mordecai learned of the plot and told the beautiful Queen Esther, his cousin, about it. Immediately, the queen told King Ahasueros what Mordecai had overheard.

The king sent investigators to find out if Mordecai's story was true. When they discovered that it was, Ahasueros ordered that the two palace guards be put to death.

Some time later, King Ahasueros promoted Haman, one of his officers, to be the prime minister of the kingdom. The king ordered all people near the royal palace to bow down to Haman, as a sign of respect for his high office.

Mordecai refused.

"Why do you disobey the king's order?" Mordecai was asked.

"I am a Jew!" said Mordecai. "I bow and kneel before no one except my God!"

When Haman heard what Mordecai had said, he was very irritated. And to get revenge, Haman made up his mind to kill Mordecai and all the other Jews in the kingdom.

One night, King Ahasueros could not fall asleep. So he asked one of his attendants to bring out the Book of Records and to read it aloud.

When it came to the part describing how Mordecai the Jew had saved the king's life, Ahasueros asked, "What honor has been given Mordecai for this wonderful deed?"

"Nothing at all has been done for him," replied the king's servant.

כָּכָה יֵעָשֶׂה
לָאִישׁ אֲשֶׁר
הַמֶּלֶךְ
חָפֵץ בִּיקָרוֹ

THUS SHALL BE DONE FOR THE MAN WHOM THE KING WISHES TO HONOR

Esther 6:9

At that very moment, someone entered the outer court of the palace.

"Who is in the court?" asked the king.

"Your Majesty, it is Haman," the guards answered.

"Please, let him enter," said the king.

As Haman approached, Ahasueros asked him: "What shall be done for a man whom the king wishes to honor?"

Which person would the king want to honor more than me? thought Haman.

"Let the man whom the king wishes to honor be dressed in royal robes, the kind worn by the king," Haman said proudly to King Ahasueros. "Let the man mount the king's royal horse," continued Haman, "and let him be led through the streets of the city. And whoever shall see him shall cry out, 'This is what is done for the man whom the king wishes to honor!'"

"You have spoken well," said the king to Haman. "Quick! Bring out royal clothes and a royal horse and honor Mordecai the Jew. Do everything that you have suggested!"

Haman's face turned pale. *How dare the king honor Mordecai the Jew! I am the one who deserves the honor!*

The wicked Haman was powerless. He had no choice but to carry out the king's command. And so, he dressed Mordecai in royal robes and mounted him on a royal horse. And then Haman, completely humiliated, took the reigns of the horse and led Mordecai the Jew through the streets of Shushan, shouting at the top of his voice: "Thus shall be done for the man whom the king wishes to honor!"

Three Friends in a Fiery Furnace

WHEN NEBUCHADNEZZAR, King of Babylonia, ruled over Jerusalem, he needed bright young men to serve in his royal court. In the Kingdom of Judah, in the southern part of the Land of Israel, he found Daniel and his three friends—Hananiah, Michael, and Azariah.

The four men were brought to Babylonia, where the Aramaic language was spoken, and the king gave them new Aramaic names. Hananiah was named Shadrach. Michael was named Meshach. And Azariah was called Abed-nego. Daniel was given the name Beltshazzar.

One day, while Daniel was away on a trip to a neighboring country, King Nebuchadnezzar made a statue of pure gold and ordered everyone to bow down to it. Shadrach, Meshach, and Abed-nego ignored the king's command. They refused to bow down to any idol.

שַׁדְרַךְ מֵישַׁךְ וַעֲבֵד נְגוֹ

SHADRACH, MESHACH, AND ABED-NEGO

Daniel 3:13

When King Nebuchadnezzar was told about this, he ordered that the three young men be brought before him.

"Is it true," the king stormed, "that you have refused to bow down to my statue of gold?"

"It is true!" said the men proudly. "We are permitted to worship only our God. We do not worship idols. It is against our religion."

"I order you to worship the statue I have erected," the king instructed. "If you refuse, you shall be thrown into a fiery furnace!"

"We are not afraid," the three men replied. "Our God will save us."

Nebuchadnezzar was in a rage. "How dare you refuse to obey me!" he exclaimed.

The king then ordered that a furnace be fired up to seven times its usual heat. He then commanded some of the strongest men in his army to bind the hands and feet of Shadrach, Meshach, and Abed-nego and to throw them into the blazing furnace.

The king's command was obeyed at once.

The next day, Nebuchadnezzar came to see what had happened to the three young men who had refused to bow down or worship the statue of gold. The king couldn't believe his eyes. The men looked no different. Not even one hair on their heads had been touched by fire!

"Blessed be the God of Shadrach, Meshach, and Abed-nego," said King Nebuchadnezzar. "The God of Israel is great! Only He could have saved a person from the flames of a fiery furnace."

Daniel in the Lion's Den

AFTER **NEBUCHADNEZZAR** died, Darius ruled the Kingdom of Babylonia. Daniel became the most trusted advisor of King Darius.

The other advisors of the king were jealous of Daniel. They plotted to remove him from his high position.

One day, the king's advisors suggested: "Let Your Majesty issue an order making it a crime for anyone, during the next thirty days, to pray to any god or man other than you." "And," they added, "whoever does not obey the command of the king shall be thrown into a den of hungry, vicious lions."

"A wonderful idea!" exclaimed King Darius. "I hereby order that such an announcement be made in every city and village in the land."

When Daniel learned that this proclamation had been issued, he went to the upper floor of his house and looked out of a window that faced Jerusalem, the holy city where the Temple of Solomon was erected. There, as he did each day, Daniel fell to his knees and prayed to the God of Israel.

וּרְמוֹ לְגֻבָּא
דִי אַרְיָוָתָא

AND THROW HIM INTO THE LION'S DEN

Daniel 6:17

When the king's servants saw Daniel praying to his own God, they approached Darius and said to him: "Your Majesty, is it not true that you proclaimed that no one is to worship anyone but you?"

"Yes, indeed," said Darius. "And that order must be obeyed."

"Please be advised, your Majesty," the servants continued, "that Daniel, from the Land of Judah, has ignored your order. He has been praying to his God in Jerusalem three times each day."

When King Darius heard this, he was disturbed. He loved Daniel and did not want to harm him.

After some time had passed and the king's servants saw that Daniel was not being punished, they approached the king one more time: "O, King Darius,

did you not say that anyone who violates your order will be punished?"

At first the king did not answer. But, finally, he declared: "As much as I love Daniel, he must pay for his crime. He must be thrown to the lions."

As the servants prepared to hurl Daniel into the lion's den, the king whispered to him, "Do not fear, Daniel. I am sure that the God whom you serve will save you."

Daniel was then thrown into the den of hungry, growling lions. A rock was rolled over the mouth of the den, and the king placed his seal on the rock to make sure that no one would dare move it.

The following morning, at the first light of dawn, King Darius rushed to see what had happened to Daniel.

Miracle of miracles! When the rock was removed from the mouth of the den, Daniel was sitting in a corner safe and sound. The lions had not harmed him.

King Darius was overjoyed. His favorite advisor had been saved!